D1594584

The
Pocket
Financial
Planner

The Pocket Financial Planner

Samuel D. Carey
Certified Financial Planner

BOB ADAMS, INC.
PUBLISHERS

ISBN: 1-55850-993-3

Published by Bob Adams, Inc., 260 Center Street, Holbrook, Massachusetts, 02343.

Printed in the United States of America.

ABOUT THE AUTHOR

Sam Carey is a Certified Financial Planner and registered Investment Adviser active in the training field. In this book, he combines his technical experience in finance, management, and training with his psychological experience in counseling and group facilitation. Experience has shown this to be a meaningful combination, since many financial difficulties are based in life situations and promoted by human behavior.

Sam is a Senior Associate with Margo Murray-Hicks & Associates (a management training consulting firm) and president of his own financial planning firm, which specializes in fee-only financial counseling. His advanced degree in counseling (clinical) assists him in dealing with the personal issues associated with the financial needs of his clients. Sam is registered as an Investment Adviser with both the U.S. Securities & Exchange Commission and the State of California.

Acknowledgments

Grateful thanks are extended to Kate Layzer and Elizabeth Tragert for their assistance in the preparation of this manuscript.

Dedicated to your financial future.

CONTENTS

Section 2:
Where Do I Want To Go?/79

Section Three:
How Will I Get There?/103

Conclusion/140

PREFACE

    This book is about life's choices, some of which are financial.

    It is designed both for self-study and for use in a group process facilitated by a financial planner. Self-directed, introspective questions and exercises are included to complement the issues and to promote an awareness of what choices are open to the participant. An effort is made to show how the reader's previous choices have resulted in his/her present situation and what choices (financial and otherwise) are needed to arrive at where s/he wants to be in the future. This is financial planning.

    Joint planning by two people in a relationship is encouraged. The exercises, however, should be completed separately to call attention to the inevitable differences between the two. This could be a first step in helping couples improve how they discuss and plan together.

YOUR
CHOICES
MAKE
THE
DIFFERENCE!

INTRODUCTION

Each of us is born with a predisposition to make choices in a certain way. As we are conditioned and shaped by the events of our lives, the process by which we make choices becomes more complex. From this combination of predisposition and conditioning, we develop the unique set of habits, preferences, beliefs, desires, values, myths, and dreams that we sometimes call "tendencies." Since our tendencies determine what we believe to be desirable and proper, they also influence what we think we want and, subsequently, our choices.

Financial planning choices are a subset of life choices and are influenced by the same predispositions, conditioning, habits, preferences, beliefs, desires, values, myths, and dreams. Our present financial situation (favorable or unfavorable) is largely the result of our previous financial planning choices. To have any hope of improving such choices in the future will require a degree of education, training, and commitment to different ways of functioning and thinking.

This workbook on financial planning choices has two basic purposes.

1. To present financial planning choices not as separate from life's choices but as supplementary to and consistent with life's choices. In other words, financial planning is the planning necessary to finance life objectives.

2. To help you, the reader, learn the discipline of creative financial planning: to evaluate where you are now in order to build your planning process on firm ground, to think through your life and financial goals, to develop a plan to accomplish your goals and objectives, and to make commitments and act accordingly.

At the end of this workbook is a financial planning form. The form is also reproduced earlier on the following page, along with a sample plan. This sample financial plan should give you an idea of where this workbook will lead you. The workbook is organized as a friendly, personal guide. Please refer to the Workbook Maps located at the beginning of each section for a menu of the material that follows.

SAMPLE OF A PLAN USING
THE "FINANCIAL PLANNING FORM"

1. Specific goals or objectives to be accomplished

    > *Remodel kitchen next year: $5,000 for materials if I do my own labor.*

    Priority of this objective
    1st <u>X</u> 2nd   3rd   4th

2. Present situation:

    > *Spending all of income.*
    > *Have no savings or emergency fund.*
    > *Have accumulated $3,000 in credit card debt.*

    Dollar amount presently available for this objective:

    $ <u>*None*</u>

    Source of funds:

    ――――

3. Constraint analysis for this objective

Time:	*As soon as possible.*
Liquidity:	*High--need cash, can't afford to lose principal.*
Marketability:	*High--need cash quickly.*
Tax Consequences:	*Important.*
Risk tolerance:	*Very low.*
Diversification:	*Important.*
Social responsibility:	*Not applicable.*

4. Plan to accomplish this goal
   (Date goals to be accomplished in parentheses)

   a) Control spending with a new budget
      and bookkeeping system. Balance
      spending to income, permitting
      a $500 per month savings.
      *(Date to be accomplished: one month
      from now.)*

   b) Eliminate debt of $3,000.
      *(Date to be accomplished: six months
      from now.)*

   c) Establish emergency fund at $4,000.
      Place in interest checking
      account to avoid bank service
      charges.
      *(Date to be accomplished: two years
      from now.)*

   d) Remodel kitchen, paying $5,000 cash.
      Place $5,000 in money market
      account to keep available with
      higher interest.
      *(Date to be accomplished: two years
      from now.)*

e) Be on lookout for necessary
   materials on sale
   (no credit purchases).
   *(Date to be accomplished: after
   one year.)*

5. Performance on objective will be measured:
   in 2 mos.

6. Dollar amount of resources available for
   less priority goals:

   $ _None_
   Source of funds:

7. Do you want to revise this plan to accommodate other lower priority goals?

   Yes: No: <u>X</u>

WHERE
AM I
NOW?

1.0 "WHERE AM I NOW?" OVERVIEW

Where you are now is the result of the choices you have made so far. In this section we are going to look at your spending patterns, your preferences, your responsibilities, your failures, and your successes. Future growth and future choices need a firm foundation to build on. Part of building a firm foundation is understanding and accepting "where you are now."

In this section you will observe that you have tendencies that promote growth, a-chievement, and well being. You will also note tendencies that do not promote your future well being. It will take discipline to emphasize the former and minimize the latter.

Our purpose here is not to establish guilt for past actions but to determine what future actions will be necessary to accomplish your goals. In each of the five sub-sections of this section there will be "reflection" items that will include asking you to note what you like best about your present situation and what items need the most work.

1.1 WORKBOOK MAP
SECTION 1: "WHERE AM I NOW?"

CONSIDERING MY
PREFERENCES
1.2

CONSIDERING MY
LIFE LINE
1.3

CONSIDERING MY
PERSONAL
DATA
1.4

KEEPING TRACK
(CONSIDERING
BUDGETING)
1.5

CONSIDERING SOME
RULES FOR SUCCESS
1.6

1.2 MY PREFERENCES

We will begin by reflecting upon your preferences. Preferences are the way you tend to feel and act. For this exercise, do not consider your preferences right or wrong. The purpose is to reflect on "where you are."

For each of the following preferences, select a value from 1 to 9 that best describes your usual functioning between the two positions noted.

I try to control my life.

1 2 3 4 5 6 7 8 9

Life events mostly just happen.

(For example: 1 or 2 would indicate a strong desire for control; 8 or 9 indicates a laid back life style; 3 to 7 are various positions in between.)

I do not like risks.

1 2 3 4 5 6 7 8 9

I often take chances.

Security is very important to me.

1 2 3 4 5 6 7 8 9

I am comfortable with the unknown.

I consult others on issues in my life.

1 2 3 4 5 6 7 8 9

I tend to make my own choices.

I always manage to put money away.

1 2 3 4 5 6 7 8 9

I never have money saved.

I like to win.

1 2 3 4 5 6 7 8 9

Being in the game is more important.

I know how much I spend . . . I'm organized.

1 2 3 4 5 6 7 8 9

Where does the money go . . . I'm disorganized.

I want lots of information before I take action.

1 2 3 4 5 6 7 8 9

I rely on feelings.

I understand the tax laws.

1 2 3 4 5 6 7 8 9

I do not understand the tax laws.

I am willing to save for the future.

1 2 3 4 5 6 7 8 9

I want it now!

1.21 REFLECTIONS ON "MY PREFERENCES"

1. In the spaces provided, write down how your indicated preferences may affect your financial choices.

Being in control (For example: "I prefer to control my investments myself."):

Fear of risking:

Security:

Need to be dependent or independent:

Need to save or spend:

Need to win:

Being organized or disorganized:

Information vs. feeling:

Knowledge of tax laws:

Delayed satisfaction:

2.   State two observations about your preferences that you feel satisfied with and do not wish to change.

a)

b)

3.   State two observations about your preferences that you feel dissatisfied with and wish to change.

a)

b)

1.3 MY LIFE LINE

Birth   Death

0----------------20---------------40----------------60----------------80

                                              or later

Insert a   "(^)"   where your age is on your life line.

Zero to twenty: development years.

Twenty to forty: establishment years.

Forty to sixty: productive years.

Sixty and above: retirement years.

Following are typical events that occur during a person's lifetime. Consider the events in your life while answering the questions that follow.

0 to 20 years: (Development)		
	a)	Childhood
	b)	School
	c)	First love
	d)	First job
	e)	Breaking away
	f)	Education, training for future

20 to 40 years: (Establishment)		
	a)	Begin career
	b)	Establish career/personal goals
	c)	Marriage (divorce, remarriage)
	d)	Children
	e)	Purchase home
	f)	Community interaction

40 to 60 years: (Productive)	a) Increased earnings potential
	b) Increased job responsibility
	c) Rethink career/personal goals
	d) Grandchildren
	e) Plan for retirement
	f) Reflect upon meaning of life
60 to death: (Retirement)	a) Phase out work/earning efforts
	b) Develop neglected parts of self
	c) Satisfy desires to see/do
	d) Life pace slower/health poorer
	e) Contribute to social causes
	f) Contribute to family well being

1.31 REFLECTIONS ON "MY LIFE LINE"

1. What is the number of years until your retirement?

2. What is your monthly retirement income objective? $

3. List goals that you want to accomplish prior to retirement.

   a)

   b)

   c)

4. Do you have a will? Yes___ No___

5. List choices you have made that have most increased your earnings potential.

   Development years:

   Establishment years:

   Productive years:

6. List choices you have made that have most decreased your earnings potential.

Development years:

Establishment years:

Productive years:

7. List choices you have made that have brought you the most satisfaction or joy.

Development years:

Establishment years:

Productive years:

8. List choices that you made that have brought you the least satisfaction or joy.

Development years:

Establishment years:

Productive years:

1.4 MY PERSONAL DATA

When you go to a doctor to get medical advice, or to an attorney to get legal advice, or to a loan officer for a loan, you begin by reviewing your personal history. Personal information is also important in financial planning; it details your present responsibilities, assets, and liabilities.

Complete the following two pages of personal data. While doing so, keep note of areas that are important for your future goal setting and financial planning.

Worry about
your ability
and
competence,
not about
money.

Money tends
to come when
you are doing
the right
thing for
you.

1.41   REVIEW OF "MY PERSONAL DATA"

1.   YOURSELF

Today's date:

Name:

Address:

Age: Sex:

Social Security No.:

Home Phone:

Business Phone:

Occupation:

Business Address:

Present Marital Status:

2. SPOUSE

Name:

Age: Sex:

Social Security No.:

Occupation:

Business Address:

Phone:

3. DEPENDENTS

Name:

Age:

Name:

Age:

Name:

Age:

Name:

Age:

4. INSURANCE   (Company, type, amount)

Life:

Home:

Car:

Hospitalization:

Disability:

Umbrella:

5. MISCELLANEOUS

Tax-filing status:

Who does your taxes?

Do you have a will?

Do you own a home?   Rent?

Monthly Payment:

Health problems in family:

Are any of your assets earmarked for future use?

Job Income: (Both you and your spouse, all sources)

<u>Position</u>   <u>Salary/yr.</u>

Other Income:

<u>Sources</u>   <u>Amount/yr.</u>

Real Estate (start with home):

		Amount
<u>Address</u>	<u>Payment/mo.</u>	<u>Owed</u>

Market <u>Value</u>		Yearly <u>Income</u>

Savings/Stock:

Type   Location

Current   Yearly
Value   Income

Other Assets:

Type   Location

Value   Income/yr.

Non-Real Estate Loans/Debt
(including credit card balances)

Source	Payment/mo.	Amt. Owed

Other Liabilities (Alimony, child support, parent support):

Type	Amount/mo.	Amount/yr.

Note: net worth equals total assets less total liabilities.

1.43 REFLECTIONS ON "MY PERSONAL DATA"

1. List two items in your personal data that indicate satisfactory financial planning.

> a)

> b)

2. List two items in your personal data that indicate a lack of financial planning.

> a)

> b)

3. How might you build on the satisfactory items in the future?

What will you do first?

When?

4. How might you improve upon the items that were not satisfactory?

What will you do first?

When?

"If the government can't balance its budget, why do I have to?"

1.5 KEEPING TRACK

Keeping track of your spending, earning, and saving patterns with a budget or some other control system is quite distasteful to many people.   My experience has shown, however, that those who are out of control financially often do not know where their money goes. Even those who think they know are usually surprised by the facts when an analysis is made. If you do know where your money has gone, then you are in control of your financial life. Meaningful plans for the future are dependent upon an awareness of your present spending habits and patterns.

Even those who resist any real "budgeting" efforts will be enlightened by a simple twelve month income/spending analysis.   Use a form similar to the one that follows.   Change the categories to fit your lifestyle and spending patterns.   The purpose is to group your spending into dollar categories large enough to estimate (and control) easily.

Instructions:

1.   Inflows (income) should be gross for the past year from all income sources. Do not start by using take-home earnings.

2.   Outflows should be for the same period. Use a full twelve months to cover all annual events, savings, taxes, etc.

3.   Indicate your savings.   Regular savings are recommended to build an emergency fund (three months of your average spending is suggested) and to finance your future goals and objectives.   Pay yourself first.

4.   Observe that there are two groups of spending: fixed outflows and variable outflows.   Fixed outflows include all regular expense items, such as taxes, home and car payments, and utilities--i.e., items that do not change frequently.

5.   Variable outflows include all other spending categories that reflect your lifestyle.   Do not make categories for small dollar amounts.

6.   Balance your inflows and outflows for the twelve months.

7.   Once you have completed your analysis of the previous twelve months, you may wish to project what the next year's income and spending budget will be. Do not forget savings. Balance inflows and outflows.

8.   Use the form on that follows for the above exercise.

For those who own a personal computer, there are many bookkeeping and budgeting software packages available that can facilitate the record keeping and calculations involved-- and can make the tasks more fun.

1.51 TWELVE-MONTH INFLOW/OUTFLOW FORMS

ACTUAL INFLOWS FOR
PERIOD FROM _____ TO _____

a) Salaries
b) Interest/dividends
c) Rental income
d) Annuities/retirement
e) Social security
f) Business income
g) Unemployment/disability
h) Alimony/child support
i) Sale of assets income
j) Other

Total Inflows: _____

ACTUAL OUTFLOWS FOR
PERIOD FROM _____ TO _____

Savings and Investments
   a)   IRA/Keogh/retirement
   b)   College fund
   c)   Emergency fund
   d)   Other

   Total Savings
      and Investments: _____

Fixed Outflows
   a)   Home payment/rent
   b)   Other real estate payments
   c)   Auto/boat payments
   d)   Insurance
   e)   Property taxes
   f)   Other taxes
   g)   Utilities
   h)   Other

   Total Fixed Outflows: _____

Variable Outflows
   a)   Food/eating out
   b)   Personal money
   c)   Transportation
   d)   Clothes/personal care
   e)   Medical/dental
   f)   Entertainment/vacations

g) Education
h) Household expenses
i) Licenses/dues/fees
j) Gifts/Christmas
k) Capital spending
l) Major home/auto repairs
m) Payments to reduce debt
n) Other

Total Variable Outflows: _____

TOTAL OUTFLOWS: _____

Available Cash or
   Increased Debt: _____

PROJECTED INFLOWS FOR
PERIOD FROM ____ TO ____

a) Salaries
b) Interest/dividends
c) Rental income
d) Annuities/retirement
e) Social security
f) Business income
g) Unemployment/disability
h) Alimony/child support
i) Sale of assets income
j) Other

    Total Inflows: _____

PROJECTED OUTFLOWS FOR
PERIOD FROM _____ TO _____

Savings and Investments
   a)   IRA/Keogh/retirement
   b)   College fund
   c)   Emergency fund
   d)   Other

   Total Savings
      and Investments: _____

Fixed Outflows
   a)   Home payment/rent
   b)   Other real estate payments
   c)   Auto/boat payments
   d)   Insurance
   e)   Property taxes
   f)   Other taxes
   g)   Utilities
   h)   Other

   Total Fixed Outflows: _____

Variable Outflows
   a)   Food/eating out
   b)   Personal money
   c)   Transportation
   d)   Clothes/personal care
   e)   Medical/dental
   f)   Entertainment/vacations

g) Education
h) Household expenses
i) Licenses/dues/fees
j) Gifts/Christmas
k) Capital spending
l) Major home/auto repairs
m) Payments to reduce debt
n) Other

Total Variable Outflows: _____

TOTAL OUTFLOWS: _____

Available Cash or
    Increased Debt: _____

1.52 POINTS TO REMEMBER ABOUT "KEEPING TRACK"

1.   Budgets work best when each person has a certain amount of personal money not accounted for by item or purchase. Personal money can be for lunches, small purchases, gifts, etc. and should be accounted for in total for the month or week.

2.   The purpose of a budget is not to make life confining or difficult.   The purpose is to know where your money is being spent and to give you the option of making desired changes.

3.   When money is tight, use your budget to make impulse purchases difficult in order to keep spending within available funds.

4.   Maintain a cash-spending basis. Pay off credit card purchases every month.   The goal is to pay no interest charges, except for home (and, if necessary, car) payments.

5. Keep separate track of tax-deductible items as part of your spending control system.

6. Keep track of spending within each of your spending categories. It is best to make entries in your system when you make the purchase or when you withdraw an amount from your system, not at the end of the month. It is important to develop an awareness of how you are doing with regard to your budget objectives throughout the month.

7. One effective recording method is to use a separate page in a ledger for each budget category. Make entries as the activity occurs. Also keep a separate envelope for receipts relating to each ledger page.

8. While it is true that you need a budgeting system that is workable for your family, it is also true that each family usually needs one person who is responsible for keeping the system current and effective.

9.   Monthly budgets are more difficult to establish than merely dividing your annual budget by twelve.   Some months include amounts to cover taxes, vacations, school clothes, etc.   For monthly budgets, use a large spreadsheet with a column for each spending category.   Make daily entries of amounts spent and available to be spent.   This exercise is time-consuming at first, but after a while you will learn where your trouble spots are and can concentrate your efforts in those areas.

10. Keep your system current.

1.53 REFLECTING ON "KEEPING TRACK"

1. Did you resist the "Keeping Track" process?

   Yes   No

   If you did, why?

   Will you overcome this resistance?

   Yes   No

2. List three spending categories that appear to be under control.

   a)

   b)

   c)

3. List three spending categories that most need improvement.

a)

b)

c)

What steps will you take to bring each of these spending categories under control?

a)   When?

b)   When?

c)   When?

4. Will you commit to saving a fixed percentage of your income?

     Yes   No

    What percent?   When will you start?

5. What future desires do you have that will require a savings program now to provide the necessary funds?

    a)

    b)

    c)

1.6 RULES FOR SUCCESS

Following is a list of attitudes, habits, and rules of thumb that many financially successful people have found to be valuable. Consider whether these are consistent with your usual ways of doing things.

1. *Start now*--do not procrastinate.

2. *Establish life goals*--support them with financial planning.

3. *Learn to manage money.* Spend less than you earn. Save regularly.

4. *Learn the tax laws.*

5. *Get the right kind of life insurance.* (Consider term policies instead of whole life.)

6. *Acquire equity.* (Buy a home and other assets. Owning equity has been the key to wealth for most Americans.)

7. *Keep money in proper perspective.*

8. *Do what you like;* know what you do; do it well.

9. *Develop a winning mentality.*

a) *Attitude*--be positive, think positive, support others.

b) *Luck*--luck will happen with necessary preparation.

c) *Truth*--base decisions on facts, not desires or preferences.

d) *Concentrate efforts*--use your intelligence; use professionals.

e) *Pay fairly* for what you get from others--avoid trying to get something for nothing.

f) *Be enthusiastic*--enthusiasm is contagious; it creates opportunities.

g) *Think,* don't guess--acquire essential information.

h) *Build capital*--start as young as possible.

i) Believe in yourself--do not be overly impressed by the opinions of others.

j) *Persist*--successful people persist.

k) *Make decisions*--making decisions is a privilege.

l) *Do not be too cautious*--there are few rewards without risks.

m) *Develop self-discipline*--this is the basis of savings, goal attainment.

n) *Have expectations*--winners expect to win.

1.61 REFLECTIONS ON RULES FOR SUCCESS

1. Each row represents one of the rules you have just read. Place a check in the column that fits you best, based on your reaction to the ideas listed on the previous page.

	No Problem	Occasional Problems	Need Work
1			
2			
3			
4			
5			
6			
7			
8			

The Pocket Financial Planner

	No Problem	Occasional Problems	Need Work
9a			
9b			
9c			
9d			
9e			
9f			
9g			
9h			
9i			
9j			
9k			
9l			
9m			
9n			
Total:			

2.   List the three *RULES FOR SUCCESS* that you feel you follow best.

   a)

   b)

   c)

3.   List the three *RULES FOR SUCCESS* that you feel you need to work hardest to master in order to improve your chances for success. Also indicate what you might do to improve this situation.

   a)   Rule:

       What I can do:

   b)   Rule:

       What I can do:

   c)   Rule:

       What I can do:

Congratulations! If you have completed the exercises up to this point, you have already succeeded in pinpointing your specific strengths--and those areas that could use more work. You're well on the way to more effective planning.

WHERE DO I WANT TO GO?

2. "WHERE DO I WANT TO GO?"
INTRODUCTION

Goal setting time! Dream time, to be sure, but the dreams in question must be measurable, attainable ones, based on where you are now and what you want to commit your life to in the future. Old habits may need to be adjusted. Action will be required. Such courses may be difficult, but success can put you in control of your financial life.

2.1 WORKBOOK MAP
SECTION 2: "WHERE DO I WANT TO GO?"

CONSIDERING RULES FOR
MORE EFFECTIVE GOALS
2.2

SETTING INITIAL GOALS
2.3

REFLECTING ON GOAL
EFFECTIVENESS
2.4

CONSIDERING "NEEDS WORK"
ITEMS FROM SECTION 1.2
2.5

FINALIZING GOALS
2.6

2.2 *TEN RULES FOR MORE EFFECTIVE* ᴜᴄ

Listed below are ten rules for making goal setting more effective. Apply each rule to your goals in order to make them as effective as possible. Effective goals will:

1. *Be defined.* Goals such as "to be happy" are not specific or well defined. It is particularly true that financial goals need to be quite specific to be effective.

2. *Be attainable.* Unattainable goals give you an excellent reason for not trying.

3. *Be difficult.* Goals that are too easy are a cop-out.

4. *Be measurable.* Measurable goals will keep you on the right track next month, next year.

5. *Force choices.* When you cannot have everything, what will you choose? Can you separate your "needs" from your "wants"? Effective goals will force you to choose.

6. *Be complementary to life's purpose.* Effective life goals will support your life's purpose; effective financial goals will finance your life's goals.

7. *Not be in conflict with things you want.*
If you want things to stay as they are, you will
not make the choices necessary to change them.

8. *Conform with your ideas of what is
"proper."* Few of us will struggle against our
inner integrity.

9. *Be for more than money.* Money may be
necessary to accomplish a goal, but a goal of
simply attaining money leaves out your life
objectives.

10. *Be what you value and will commit to.*
Commitment is the key to accomplishing your
goals

2.3 INITIAL GOAL SETTING

Establishing personal life and financial goals and   objectives is a difficult and complex activity.   Our next activity will help you to put your goals in writing.   Use the form that follows.   This initial attempt at goal development will serve as the basis for review and further consideration.

Although it will be difficult, the act of writing down your goals is the first step in developing commitment.   Commitment will help you make those choices that will make your goals materialize.   Keep this in mind as you set about putting your goals and objectives on paper.

1. Decide on your goal.

2. Establish a clear mental picture of your goal.

3. Reflect on this mental picture often.

4. Give your goal positive energy.

GOAL AND OBJECTIVE FORM

1. What is the principal *PURPOSE* of your life?

2. What are your *LIFE* goals and objectives?

    a)   For the next two years:

         1.

         2.

         3.

    b)   For two to five years from now:

         1.

         2.

    c)   For five or more years from now:

         1.

         2.

3. What are your *FINANCIAL* goals and objectives?

    a)   For the next two years:

        1.

        2.

        3.

    b)   For two to five years from now:

        1.

        2.

    c)   For five or more years from now:

        1.

        2.

2.4 REFLECTIONS ON EFFECTIVE GOAL SETTING

Reflect on your initial goals by using the recap forms below. Score the effectiveness of each of your goal sections as follows:

> 0 - My goals are not effective in this area.

> 1 - My goals need additional work to be effective.

> 2 - My goals are close to being effective.

> 3 - My goals are effective in this area.

Life Goals

	Next 2 yrs.	2-5 yrs.	Over 5 yrs.
Defined			
Attainable			
Difficult			
Measurable			
Force Choices			
Complement Purpose			
Avoid Conflict			
Proper			
More than Money			
Commitment			
Totals:			

Number rated 0: ____

Number rated 1: ____

Number rated 2: ____

Number rated 3: ____

Financial Goals

	Next 2 yrs.	2-5 yrs.	Over 5 yrs.
Defined			
Attainable			
Difficult			
Measurable			
Force Choices			
Complement Purpose			
Avoid Conflict			
Proper			
More than Money			
Commitment			
Totals:			

Number rated 0: _____
Number rated 1: _____
Number rated 2: _____
Number rated 3: _____

The process you have just completed is often a discouraging one, since few of us have effectively thought through our lives and financial goals. In any case, you now have two choices.

1. Stop here and let things remain as they have been.

2. Commit yourself to a planning process that includes establishing effective goals and taking action on the planned decision.

If you chose to commit yourself to planning, the exercises that follow should help you on your way.

2.5 REFLECTIONS ON "WHERE AM I NOW?" NEEDS WORK ITEMS

In section 1, WHERE AM I NOW, you listed some areas in your life that "need work." It can be useful to consider how these "need work" habits and attitudes may affect your selection of goals. Are you continuing to avoid facing these issues? Will your goals reflect consideration of ways to improve in these areas?

1. How might the habits and attitudes that "need work" affect your goal-setting process?

a)   Preferences:

b)   Life-line choices:

c)   Personal data:

d)   Keeping track:

e)   Rules for success:

2. If you do change these "needs work" features of your life, how will such changes help you achieve future goals and objectives?

3. Did you resist dealing with your "needs work" items?

Yes_____ No_____

Is this resistance likely to impede action to achieve your goals and objectives?

Yes_____ No_____

2.6 FINAL GOAL SETTING

It is now time to review and finalize your goals and objectives. Another "Goal and Objective" form follows. Consider the following as you approach this task:

1. Is your life purpose supported by your life goals? Do your financial goals support your life goals?

2. Have you considered each of the ten rules for effective goal setting for each of your goals?

3. Have you considered your tendencies that "need work" in your goal setting?

4. *WILL YOU COMMIT TO THESE GOALS?*

Living well doesn't necessarily depend on having more money and things; another way is to simplify your life.

GOAL AND OBJECTIVE FORM

1. What is the principal *PURPOSE* of your life?

2. What are your *LIFE* goals and objectives?

    a)   For the next two years:

         1.

         2.

         3.

    b)   For two to five years from now:

         1.

         2.

    c)   For five or more years from now:

         1.

         2.

3. What are your *FINANCIAL* goals and objectives?

    a)   For the next two years:

        1.

        2.

        3.

    b)   For two to five years from now:

        1.

        2.

    c)   For five or more years from now:

        1.

        2.

HOW WILL I GET THERE?

3. HOW WILL I GET THERE?
OVERVIEW

The financial-planning process includes the following steps:

1.   Gather data and information (covered in section 1:   WHERE AM I NOW?)

2.   Evaluate present situations (covered in section 1:   WHERE AM I NOW?)

3.   Establish and reflect on life goals (covered in section 2:   WHERE DO I WANT TO GO?)

4.   Establish financial goals and objectives to complement life goals (covered in section 2: WHERE DO I WANT TO GO?)

5.   Develop a financial plan based on present situations and established goals (covered in the following pages--section 3:   HOW WILL I GET THERE?)

Any financial plan will require commitment and action on the part of the individual.   Implement the developed plan.   You may require professional assistance to implement your plan.

If your situation changes, or if the plan is not working, goal and plan changes may be required.   Monitor the plan.

As noted above, this section will focus on the development of your financial plan. A financial plan is a scheme for accomplishing the goals that are selected with the resources that are available. Your plan should be based on your present situation (WHERE AM I NOW?) and on your established goals (WHERE DO I WANT TO GO?). It must also consider applicable financial constraints, priorities, and risk and return relationships. These will be reviewed next.

3.1 WORKBOOK MAP
SECTION 3: "HOW WILL I GET THERE?"

CONSIDERING FINANCIAL
PLANNING CONSTRAINTS
3.2

CONSIDERING PLANNING
PRIORITIES
3.3

CONSIDERING RISK VS.
RETURN
3.4

EVALUATING AVAILABLE
PROFESSIONAL HELP
3.5

USING THE FINANCIAL
PLANNING FORM
3.6

DEVELOPING YOUR OWN
FINANCIAL PLANS

3.2 FINANCIAL PLANNING CONSTRAINTS

The financial planning constraints listed below are items that may limit your choice of investment or approach and that should be considered in your planning process.

1. **TIME HORIZON:** A time horizon is the time in which a specific financial goal is expected to be attained--or it is the holding period for an investment. The time horizon for each goal will influence the selection of investment vehicles and amounts. Indeed, if a goal cannot be attained because the desired return is not achievable or because there are insufficient resources available, the goal or time horizon must be modified.

2. **LIQUIDITY:** Liquidity is the ability to readily convert an investment into cash without losing any of the principal invested. Lower expected return is usually associated with highly liquid investments such as insured savings accounts.

3. **MARKETABILITY:** Marketability is the degree to which there is an active market in which an investment can readily be traded. Limited marketability makes investments more risky than usual; consequently, such investments should offer above-average return (spec-

ulative corporate bonds, for example).

4. **TAX CONSEQUENCES**: Money made is one thing. Money available after taxes is another--and more important. Tax planning should be a continuing activity, not just a year-end ordeal.

5. **RISK TOLERANCE**: Your risk tolerance level is an intangible and personal constraint based on your emotional temperament and attitudes. The level of risk an individual is willing to assume affects the level of return that individual can expect.

6. **DIVERSIFICATION**: Diversification is the risk-reducing strategy of not putting all your investments into one vehicle or institution. Diversification reduces the risk exposure to any one market condition.

7. **SOCIAL RESPONSIBILITY**: Do you want to support a product or cause with your investment? Do you want to avoid investments associated with any product, cause, or location?

3.21 REFLECTIONS ON
"FINANCIAL PLANNING CONSTRAINTS"

Consider how these financial planning constraints might affect your plan or proposed investment.

1. **Time** (When will you need the money?)

2. **Liquidity** (Will you need cash quickly without loss of principal?)

3. **Marketability** (Are there places to sell your investment without delay or penalty?)

4. **Tax Consequences** (What is your current tax rate?)

5. *Risk Tolerance* (Can you endure the chance of a principal loss for the chance of a higher gain?)

6. *Diversification* (Are all your investments in the same item, market, or security?)

7. *Social Responsibility* (Do you wish to support something with your investment?)

3.3 PLANNING PRIORITIES

Listed below are some practical steps that should be given priority in the development of your financial plan.

1. **GET CONTROL OF YOUR SPENDING.** The very first step in any successful financial planning effort is to be in control of your spending habits. This usually necessitates the following initiatives.

a) Keeping spending within the limits of your income.

b) Paying yourself by regular savings. (Saving at least ten percent of your total income is recommended.)

c) Keeping your bookkeeping system current so that you can identify where you are with regard to your planned spending at any time.

d) Avoiding the credit trap. Pay all credit purchases (except your home or car payments) in full each month.

2. **CREATE AN EMERGENCY CASH FUND** equal to three months of your usual spending.

3. **BUY A HOME.** It does not have to be the home of your dreams, since you will probably sell it for a better one in five to seven years. Buying a home will be the basis of your future wealth.

4. **DIVERSIFY YOUR SAVINGS INVESTMENTS.** Avoid putting all of your savings in the same investment (except a home) or institution.

5. **UNDERSTAND AND HEED YOUR RISK-TOLERANCE LEVEL.** Investments that keep you up at night should be avoided.

6. **OBTAIN TERM INSURANCE** to cover your risk exposure. Unless you have trusted, professional, third-party advice, keep your insurance and savings programs separate.

7. **GET AND USE PROFESSIONAL ADVICE.** Augment advice from   brokerage firms selling a product with that from other trusted third-party professionals.

8. **LEARN TO DO YOUR OWN INCOME TAXES.** This will benefit your overall financial well-being. Developing an awareness of general economic conditions and what can be expected in the future is another valuable learning tool.

9. **PRIORITIZE YOUR FINANCIAL PLANNING EFFORTS.** Select the most important item you ∕ant to plan for. Plan for that. Select the second item. Plan for it. Decide if you will permit the second item to affect your planning for the first. Select the third item, and continue in this fashion.

10. If you are eligible to **FUND AN IRA** or other tax-deductible retirement plan account, be sure to give this a high priority in your planning efforts.

11. **HAVE A WILL,** unless you are satisfied that the state probate system will accomplish exactly what you want.

12. **DO NOT LOCK ALL YOUR SAVINGS ASSETS** into an investment that will cost you a penalty to withdraw in an emergency.

13. **KEEP MONEY IN PROPER PERSEPCTIVE.** Money seldom provides happiness, health, time, energy, mature relationships, or love.

"The use of money is all the advantage there is in having money."

--Benjamin Franklin

3.31 REFLECTIONS ON "PLANNING PRIORITIES"

Indicate below those suggested priority items that you intend to make part of your planning process.

1a) Spend less than is made
   I already do this ___
   This will be part of my plan ___
   This will not be part of my plan ___

 b) Maintain savings of ten percent
   I already do this ___
   This will be part of my plan ___
   This will not be part of my plan ___

 c) Keep a simple, updated book-
   keeping system
   I already do this ___
   This will be part of my plan ___
   This will not be part of my plan ___

 d) Avoid the credit trap
   I already do this ___
   This will be part of my plan ___
   This will not be part of my plan ___

2. Create an emergency fund
   I already do this ___
   This will be part of my plan ___
   This will not be part of my plan ___

3. Buy a home
   I already do this ___
   This will be part of my plan ___
   This will not be part of my plan ___

4. Diversify savings investments
   I already do this ___
   This will be part of my plan ___
   This will not be part of my plan ___

5. Adhere to risk tolerance level
   I already do this ___
   This will be part of my plan ___
   This will not be part of my plan ___

6. Cover risks with term insurance
   I already do this ___
   This will be part of my plan ___
   This will not be part of my plan ___

7. Get non-sales professional advice
   I already do this ___
   This will be part of my plan ___
   This will not be part of my plan ___

8a) Do your own taxes
   I already do this ___
   This will be part of my plan ___
   This will not be part of my plan ___

 b) Be aware of economy
   I already do this ___
   This will be part of my plan ___
   This will not be part of my plan ___

9. Prioritize planning effort
   I already do this ___
   This will be part of my plan ___
   This will not be part of my plan ___

10. Fund IRAs, etc.
   I already do this ___
   This will be part of my plan ___
   This will not be part of my plan ___

11. Have a will
   I already do this ___
   This will be part of my plan ___
   This will not be part of my plan ___

12. Avoid locking in all assets
   I already do this ___
   This will be part of my plan ___
   This will not be part of my plan ___

13. Try to keep money in proper perspective

    I already do this ___

    This will be part of my plan ___

    This will not be part of my plan ___

3.4 RISK vs. RETURN

There are two general rules associated with the relationship of investment risk to expected return from the investment.

1. The potential for higher return on your investment is usually coupled with a higher risk of principal loss. Conversely, lower risk usually carries a lower return.

2. Increased safety of principal tends to result in an increased risk of loss of purchasing power because of inflation and decreased return.

Listed on the following pages are various investments and their typical relative "projected return" and "risk of loss principal."

Investment: Insured checking and savings account
Projected return: low
Risk of loss of principal: low

Investment: EE and HH government bonds
Projected return: low
Risk of loss of principal: low

Investment: U.S. Treasury bonds
Projected return: low
Risk of loss of principal: low

Investment: U.S. Treasury notes
Projected return: moderate
Risk of loss of principal: low if held, moderate if sold

Investment: Insured Certificate of Deposit
Projected return: low
Risk of loss of principal: low

Investment: Money Market account
Projected return: low
Risk of loss of principal: low

Investment: Pension Plan account
Projected return: moderate
Risk of loss of principal: low

Investment: Home ownership
Projected return: moderate to high
Risk of loss of principal: low

Investment: Municipal bonds
Projected return: moderate
Risk of loss of principal: moderate

Investment: Balanced mutual funds
Projected return: moderate
Risk of loss of principal: moderate

Investment: High-grade bonds, preferred stock
Projected return: moderate
Risk of loss of principal: moderate

Investment: Blue chip stocks
Projected return: moderate
Risk of loss of principal: moderate

Investment: Limited partnerships
Projected return: moderate to high
Risk of loss of principal: high

Investment: Real estate investments
Projected return: moderate to high
Risk of loss of principal: moderate

Investment: Speculative stocks/bonds
Projected return: high
Risk of loss of principal: high

Investment: Options
Projected return: high
Risk of loss of principal: high

Investment: Collectibles
Projected return: high
Risk of loss of principal: high

Investment: Futures contracts
Projected return: high
Risk of loss of principal: high

Note: Seek professional advice prior to moderate- or high-risk investments.

3.41 REFLECTIONS ON "RISK vs. RETURN"

1. Describe your personal tolerance to the risk of loss of principal.

How will your risk tolerance affect your investment choices?

2. Describe your need to readily convert your investment into cash without loss of principle (liquidity).

How will liquidity affect your investment choices?

3. Describe your need to have an available market for your investment (marketability).

How will marketability affect your investment choices?

3.5 USE OF PROFESSIONAL HELP IN THE PLANNING PROCESS

The use of "outside" information sources and the ideas and assistance of trained professionals will often enhance the quality and depth of your financial planning. Care should be taken by those unskilled in financial concepts, however, to augment advice given by brokerage personnel with that of other trusted third-party professionals. (In other words, be sure to compensate for the fact that the "advice" you receive may well be a sales pitch.) Listed below are information sources and possible helpful services. Indicate those you use now and those you are considering for the future.

Information Sources to Consider

1. Newspapers, books, magazines, public television, education. (These sources provide: investment information; investment advice; economic forecasting; new ideas; major purchase information.)

> I use this source now _____

> I may use this source in the future _____

2. A financial planning professional. (This source provides: help with financial goal setting and planning; investment advice; retirement and estate planning advice; new ideas.)

> I use this source now _____

> I may use this source in the future _____

3. A CPA or accountant. (These sources provide: tax planning advice; bookkeeping support; business advice.)

> I use this source now _____

> I may use this source in the future _____

4. A credit counselor. (This source provides: help with budgeting and controlling expenses; advice on use of credit.)

> I use this source now _____

> I may use this source in the future _____

5. An attorney. (This source provides: help with wills, estate plans, contracts, and real estate exchanges; legal advice.)

> I use this source now _____

> I may use this source in the future _____

6. A real estate broker. (This source provides: assistance with home purchase and sale; advice on real estate investments; refinancing information; estimates of home value.)

> I use this source now _____

> I may use this source in the future _____

7. Tax preparation service. (This source provides help with preparation of your tax forms.)

I use this source now _____

I may use this source in the future _____

8. Insurance broker. (This source provides: advice on types of insurance available; information on costs of insurance.)

I use this source now _____

I may use this source in the future _____

General rule: if your financial plan is complicated or involves large amounts of money, seek and use professional help.

3.6 USING THE FINANCIAL PLANNING FORM

1.   It is important to use the "Financial Planning Form" found at the end of this book in your planning process.   Fill in all the blanks with the appropriate information.

2.   Prioritize your various goals and objectives. Plan for the highest-priority objective first. Then plan for the second-highest-priority objective and so on.

3.   Start from your present situation.   Do not skip steps necessary to accomplish your objective, (by, for example, allocating $5,000 before you indicate where the money will come from.)

4.   Evaluate financial planning constraints for your objective.

5.   Develop a detailed plan to accomplish your goal.   Do not skip steps.

6.   Plan to measure your performance on your objective regularly.

7.   After developing your plan, ask yourself the following questions:

Will I commit to this plan?

Will the results be what I expect?   How will I know?

What will this plan do to my lifestyle?   Do I want this?

Are there other more acceptable approaches?

What areas require professionals help?

On the next page is another sample plan to review before you attempt your own plan. Good luck in your planning process.

SAMPLE OF A PLAN USING
THE "FINANCIAL PLANNING FORM"

1. Specific goals or objectives to be accomplished:

    *Establish emergency fund of
    $5,000; have $40,000 available
    for daughter's education (fresh-
    man year five years from now;
    completing senior year eight
    years from now).*

    Priority of this objective:

    1st <u>X</u> 2nd   3rd   4th

2. Present situation:

    *No emergency fund.
    No education fund.
    No credit debt except home.*

    Dollar amount presently available for
    this objective:

    $3,000

    Source of funds:
    Blue chip stocks

3. Constraint analysis for this objective:

Time: *Emergency fund: 1 yr.*
Education: 5 yrs. (first payment of $10,000)

Liquidity: *Moderate to high.*

Marketability: *High.*

Tax Consequences: *28% tax bracket.*

Risk tolerance: *Low.*

Diversification: *Important.*

Social responsibility: *No tobacco investments.*

4. Plan to accomplish this goal:

   a) *Get control of spending with a new budget and bookkeeping system.*

   b) *Initiate savings plan: $500 per month (equals $6000 per year). This establishes emergency fund by the end of this year.*

   c) *Consider stock as first contribution to education fund. This, with periodic withdrawals from savings over daughter's time in school, yields $46,000. (Savings--less emergency fund--equals $43,000 over eight years, plus stock at current value equals $46,000.)*

   d) *Place emergency fund in interest checking account.*

   e) *Place education fund in no-load mutual stock fund.*

5. Performance on objective will be measured:

   in 6 mos.

6. Dollar amount of resources available for less priority goals:

    $Zero

    Source of funds:

7. Do you want to revise this plan to accommodate other lower priority goals?

    Yes: No: <u>X</u>

THE "FINANCIAL PLANNING FORM"

(You may make copies of this form, if necessary, for personal practice and use; sale or distribution to third parties is prohibited.)

1. Specific goals or objectives to be accomplished:

   Priority of this objective:

   1st   2nd   3rd   4th

2. Present situation:

   Dollar amount presently available for this objective:

   $ _____

   Source of funds.

3. Constraint analysis for this objective:

Time:

Liquidity:

Marketability:

Tax Consequences:

Risk tolerance.

Diversification.

Social responsibility

4. Plan to accomplish this goal:

   a)

   b)

   c)

   d)

   e)

   f)

5. Performance on objective will be measured (date):

6. Dollar amount of resources available for less priority goals:

   $

   Source of funds:

7. Do you want to revise this plan to accommodate other lower priority goals?

       Yes: No:

4. CONCLUSION

By now you know that your financial planning requires discipline and will not be accomplished satisfactorily with only a half-hearted effort on your part. As noted at the outset, where you are now is the result of many of your prior choices, and you will have to make future choices to arrive where you want to be in the future.

These choices are not easy. Any training, education, and experience that you can accumulate will certainly be an advantage. You will notice that this self-help financial planning book does not attempt to solve complicated planning issues that obviously need the assistance of a professional. Such issues include the following.

Estate planning with trusts (and related issues)

Retirement planning: annuities and distributions

Real estate investment options.

Legal contracts and advice.

Large dollar investments.

Business structure and planning.

If you have completed the exercises in this book, you have gained an awareness of a number of important issues.

1. Your present situation and tendencies. (Where Am I Now? - Section 1.)

2. Your goals and objectives. (Where Do I Want To Go - Section 2.)

3. Basic financial planning. (How Will I Get There - Section 3.)

4. The relationship between life objectives and financial objectives.

To develop an effective financial plan will require you to consider these four items regardless of the complexity of your estate and the dollar amount of your resources. Going back through the exercises now that you have a better understanding of the process may yield substantial benefits. Finally, a reminder that the planning process is a never-ending one. At the very least, an annual review of your plan is recommended.

May your future choices lead you to a better understanding and acceptance of yourself and others.